interrelated processes of belief, repentance, confession, and ultimately sanctification into the discussion.

— **Holly Allen**, PhD, Professor of Family Studies
and Christian Ministries, Lipscomb University

Dr. Strickland and Dr. Westbrook have thus done a valuable service by providing this study of the significance of baptism. Steeped in Scripture, informed by history, and packed with personal insight, *New Birth* will be a valuable resource both to those considering the call of Jesus and to those engaged in disciple making.

— **Dan Williams**, PhD, Vice President for
Church Relations, Harding University

I0157704

We have two thousand years of Christian history in our rearview mirror, yet the issues about baptism remain unsettled. While the apostle Paul argued that baptism is a source of Christian unity, far too often it continues to be a source of division. When the average believer answers the question, "Why do you believe what you believe about baptism?" the answers often sound less biblical and more like systematic theology. For those looking for more Bible and less systematic theology, this book fits the bill. It will equip more disciple makers to teach baptism from a biblical foundation.

— **Brett Andrews**, founding pastor of New Life Christian Church

To build anything that will last, one must build on a strong foundation. This book establishes the necessary doctrinal foundation for a global movement of disciple making in a clear and solid way.

— **Brandon Guindon**, founding pastor of Real Life Texas

Probably no part of the Christian life has provoked more questions—and religious debate—than baptism. What is its purpose? Why should we do it? Is it necessary for salvation? These and other questions about baptism are found in this short but packed study

on the new birth by Michael Strickland and Anessa
Westbrook. This well-written book will help those
thinking about becoming Christians and deepen the
understanding of those who are already Christians.

— **Dr. Sherry Pollard**, Professor,
Harding University

Westbrook and Strickland provide a simple but
profound explanation of the conversion experience,
beginning in faith, moving through repentance and
confession, and culminating in baptism. Rooting their
language in the teaching and practices of the early
church, they call us to see this experience in the light
of discipleship and our commitment to the Lord Jesus.
Their conclusions are eminently biblical, practical, and
God-honoring.

— **John Mark Hicks**, PhD, Professor of Theology,
Lipscomb University

Strickland and Westbrook stand with the early church
in its understanding that baptism is for remission of
sins—while making it clear that salvation is always
and only by the power of Jesus' blood. Furthermore,
their holistic treatment rescues baptism from the
misunderstanding that it is a stand-alone event;
Strickland and Westbrook weave the inherently

MICHAEL STRICKLAND
& ANESSA WESTBROOK

THE REAL LIFE THEOLOGY SERIES

NEW
BIRTH

CONVERSION
AND BAPTISM

6

In memory of Jim Brinkerhoff, who
discipled me and many others.

— Michael Strickland

To my husband, Tim, and our children, Alina, Anna,
and Theo, for your unwavering support and love.
To my parents, Ken and Ann Hobby, who believed,
supported, and equipped me on my ministry journey.

— Anessa Westbrook

CONTENTS

GENERAL
EDITORS' NOTE

When Jesus Christ saves a person, they experience a new birth. As we disciple people, we must understand and teach people what Scripture teaches about this new birth. Conversion and its relationship to baptism can be difficult to understand. Churches and friendships have even divided over their understandings and practices regarding baptism. So knowing what the Bible says about these important issues and teaching it with clarity are crucial.

Michael Strickland and Anessa Westbrook are helpful guides into this investigation of what the Scriptures have to say about the new birth.

Michael Strickland is Director of Instruction and Associate Professor of Theology and Mathematics at Amridge University. He holds a Bachelor of Mathematics and a Master of Science in Mathematics from Auburn University, a Master of Arts in Biblical Studies from

Lipscomb University, and a Doctor of Philosophy in Theology from the University of Birmingham, United Kingdom. He and his wife, Mary, live in Murfreesboro, Tennessee, with their three children: Helen, Lila Beth, and Charlie.

Anessa Westbrook is an Associate Professor of Bible and Ministry at Harding University. She holds a Master of Arts in Church Growth and a Master of Divinity from Harding School of Theology as well as a Doctor of Ministry from Fuller Theological Seminary. Her doctoral research focused on the spiritual development of women. She and her husband, Tim, live in Searcy, Arkansas, with their three adult children: Alina, Anna, and Theo.

This book expounds on the section from the Renew.org Leaders' Faith Statement called "New Birth":

> God so loved the world that he gave his one and only Son, that whoever believes in him shall not perish but have eternal life. To believe in Jesus means we trust and follow him as both Savior and Lord. When we commit to trust and follow Jesus, we express this faith by repenting from sin, confessing his name, and receiving baptism by immersion in water. Baptism, as an expression of faith, is for the remission of sins. We uphold baptism as the normative means of entry into the life of discipleship. It marks our commitment

to regularly die to ourselves and rise to live for Christ in the power of the Holy Spirit. We believe God sovereignly saves as he sees fit, but we are bound by Scripture to uphold this teaching about surrendering to Jesus in faith through repentance, confession, and baptism.

*See the full Network Faith Statements at the end of this book.

Support Scriptures: 1 Corinthians 8:6; John 3:1–9; 3:16–18; 3:19–21; Luke 13:3–5; 24:46–47; Acts 2:38; 3:19; 8:36–38; 16:31–33; 17:30; 20:21; 22:16; 26:20; Galatians 3:26–27; Romans 6:1–4; 10:9–10; 1 Peter 3:21; Romans 2:25–29; 2 Chronicles 30:17–19; Matthew 28:19–20; Galatians 2:20; Acts 18:24–26.

The following tips might help you use this book more effectively (and the other books in the *Real Life Theology* series):

1. *Five questions, answers, and Scriptures.* We framed this book around five key questions with five short answers and five notable Scriptures. This format provides clarity, making it easier to commit crucial information to memory. This format also enables the books in the *Real Life Theology* series to support our

catechism. Our catechism is a series of fixed questions and answers for instruction in church or home. In all, the series has fifty-two questions, answers, and key Scriptures. This particular book focuses on the five that are most pertinent to the new birth.

2. *Personal reflection.* At the end of each chapter are six reflection questions. Each chapter is short and intended for everyday people to read and then process. The questions help you to engage the specific teachings and, if you prefer, to journal your practical reflections.

3. *Discussion questions.* The reflection questions double as discussion-group questions. Even if you do not write down the answers, the questions can be used to stimulate group conversation.

4. *Summary videos.* You can find three to seven-minute video teachings that summarize the book, as well as each chapter, at Renew.org. These short videos can function as standalone teachings. But for groups or group leaders using the book, they can also be used to launch discussion of the reading.

May God use this book to fuel faithful and effective disciple making in your life and church.

For King Jesus,
Bobby Harrington and Daniel McCoy
General Editors, *Real Life Theology* Series

INTRODUCTION

The supreme adventure is being born.
– G. K. Chesterton, *Heretics*

The Bible uses several metaphors to describe the change that God brings about when we become disciples of Jesus. We were dead in our sins but raised with Christ (Ephesians 2:5–6). We were rescued from darkness and brought into the light (1 Peter 2:9). We were lost but now found (Luke 15:32). We were slaves to sin but set free by Jesus (Romans 6:1–3). All of these descriptions convey the drastic change that takes place when someone declares that Christ is Lord. It's not just a change in behavior, but a change in the way they view the world, the people around them, and themselves.

This book is about the meaning of this change that Jesus enables, empowers, and requires for his followers, centered around the biblical metaphor of "new birth." We strive to provide helpful teaching from the Scriptures, examples of fellow disciples, and wisdom from church history—all to better understand the new birth.

WHY IS IT CALLED THE NEW BIRTH?

THROUGHOUT HISTORY, HUMANS HAVE used the language of pregnancy and birth as a metaphor for great changes. Today, we speak of companies "giving birth" to new products, and in ancient Greece, Socrates described himself as a midwife helping new philosophers to be born. The Bible uses the concept of childbirth to describe important times of great change, such as new creation in Christ and Jesus' Second Coming (Romans 8:22; Matthew 24:8). However, the most common use of the birthing metaphor in the Bible Testament deals with the transformed life that Jesus brings when we are born again through faith in him.

Why do we use this term "new birth" to describe becoming a Christian? The phrase "born again" appears in two passages in the New Testament. In John 3, a Jewish teacher named Nicodemus came to Jesus, marveling at his miracles, and Jesus advised him, "No one can see the kingdom of God unless they are born again" (3:3). Though Nicodemus seemed puzzled, Jesus explained that to be born again was to be born of water and of Spirit (likely referring to our baptism in water when we also receive the Spirit). The other occurrence of this phrase occurs in 1 Peter 1:22–23, where Peter encourages believers that they have "purified [their] souls by [their] obedience to the truth" and that they are "born again, not of perishable seed but of imperishable" (ESV). Here, Peter is referring to the purification of baptism, when a person is born anew to live forever (of eternal "imperishable seed").

> THE BIBLE USES THE CONCEPT OF THE NEW BIRTH AS A VIVID DESCRIPTOR OF THE LIFE-CHANGING MOMENT.

Thus, the Bible uses the concept of the new birth as a vivid descriptor of the life-changing moment when a person chooses to follow Jesus.

OUR CONVERSION STORIES

LIKE MANY AMERICANS, I (Michael) was raised in a nominally Christian home. I went to church on and off during childhood in my rural Alabama town. But by the time I was a teenager, I had stopped going. When I was sixteen years old, I started dating a girl who invited me to church. While the relationship with the girl fizzled, the newfound love of a church family did not. I had never experienced the kind of open, honest friendship or the mentorship that this church offered. On July 9, 1991, I was born again in the waters of baptism.[1] The next year,

I left for Auburn University, where I first participated in campus ministry and where I eventually trained for vocational ministry. Since then, it has been my privilege to introduce people young and old to the kingdom of God, and at times to baptize them. My new birth is the beginning of God's plan for me, and to introduce others to it is the greatest privilege in the world!

I (Anessa) was raised in an active Christian home by ministry-oriented parents and grandparents. My interest in baptism came naturally to me, and I entered the waters of baptism at the age of nine. Over the years, I have talked with many who were baptized at a young age like I was and have wondered if it was too early, if they really understood what they were doing. This ignorance about baptism is similar to the lack of understanding couples often have when they say "I do" on their wedding day. They generally understand what is required in marriage, but one can never fully grasp what the marriage commitment means at first. Our understanding about it deepens with the necessary changes and sacrifices involved in marriage.

That's how it is with the new birth: Jesus doesn't expect us to have all the answers at the beginning. He just expects us to step out in faith toward him, and baptism is one of the first steps on the journey. This journey is beautiful and bursting with grace-filled vistas and provision when we find ourselves in the forest. It involves experiencing the faithfulness of God, even in the most unexpected ways. I will say that helping others, especially my children, experience God and watching them grow as they embark on this journey has been one of the highlights of my life.

1

WHY IS THE NEW BIRTH NECESSARY?

Answer: Sin separates us from God, and the decision to trust and follow Jesus is a necessary part of restoring that relationship.

For all have sinned and fall short of the glory of God.
— Romans 3:23

Are you a perfect person? Without fail, every time I've asked a group of people to raise their hands if they are perfect, no one does. Even though we often say we feel pressure to appear perfect, we seem to know that we are not. To be flawed is to be human, and we respect the humility and authenticity of those who can accept their imperfections. However, when it comes to deciding if we need to be saved, which is to acknowledge our flawed nature, some people struggle to admit their imperfections as readily. We learn in 1 John 1:8, however, "If we claim to be without sin, we deceive ourselves." Romans 3:23 says, "All have sinned and fall short of the glory of God." Sin separates us from God, and in order to restore that relationship, we need intervention.

When God created humanity, he created us in his image. However, since the Garden of Eden, we as people have struggled with giving in to our own will and sinful desires. Humanity, who bears the image of God, has not reflected his image well. We have not lived up to the standards that God intended for us. Recognizing this human struggle, God assisted by giving the Israelites the law so they might maintain a holy relationship with him. The law was to provide justification, which means the removal of sin and guilt from our hearts plus the conveyance of righteousness to our lives. The people were told to be "consecrated," a term meaning to separate out people or things for holy service and dedicating them to

God.[2] The priests were commanded to consecrate themselves (Exodus 19:22), the Levites were told to consecrate the temple (2 Chronicles 29:5), and Moses was told to consecrate the Israelites (Exodus 19:10). In the Old Testament, various avenues were used in consecration: animal sacrifices (Exodus 29:1), washing (Exodus 29:4), and anointing with oil (Exodus 29:7). This was all done in an effort to maintain holiness and relationship with God. If these things were not done, Israel was at risk of God turning away from them (Deuteronomy 23:14).

The reason God would turn away, however, was not that he was judgmental or angry, as we might be tempted to view him. Instead, it's because God is perfectly holy, and sin cannot be in his presence. In Leviticus 11:44, God says, "I am the LORD your God; consecrate yourselves and be holy, because I am holy." We should not approach him lightly. Coming into his presence involves preparation. Just as Moses was commanded to take off his sandals when approaching the burning bush, we too should be prepared to stand in the presence of God (Exodus 3:5). When we stand in his presence with our sin, the contrast highlights our shortcomings and the gap between us and God.

God allowed the people to atone for their sins through the laws and purification he commanded to Israel. However, the law was difficult to keep. It was imperfect and unable to completely bridge the gap between them and God. On its own, the law was powerless to save God's people. Romans 8:3 says, "For what the law was powerless to do because it was weakened by the flesh, God did by sending his own Son in the likeness of sinful flesh to be a sin offering." Mending the broken relationship with God caused by sin required special intervention.

MENDING THE BROKEN RELATIONSHIP WITH GOD CAUSED BY SIN REQUIRED SPECIAL INTERVENTION.

God looked forward to the time when he would have this new relationship with his people. In Jeremiah 31:31–34, God promised to make a new covenant with his people. While Israel broke their old, written covenant with God, a new covenant would be written on their hearts. He anticipated this day, saying in verse thirty-three, "I will be their God, and they will be my people." We see God's heart in his constant pursuit of Israel, as he looked forward to the day when he would remember their sins no more (Jeremiah 31:34). Hebrews 10:1 says the law was a shadow of what was to come because its repeated sacrifices could not make people perfect. Jesus also referred to the limitation of the law in Matthew 5:17, stating, "Do not think that I have come to abolish the Law or the Prophets; I have not come to abolish them but to fulfill them."

Although the recurring sacrifices could not truly cleanse people from their sin, Jesus sacrificed himself and made us holy through his sacrifice (Hebrews 10:10). Because we are made holy, we can enter into that relationship with God in which he is our God and we are his people.

After accepting our sinfulness and our need for a Savior, the next question is *how* we are saved. This question provides the backdrop of the rest of the book. In the chapters that follow, we will learn that the Bible teaches the new birth as a death-to-life matter of placing our faith in Jesus. We express this faith in Jesus by

- repenting from sin
- confessing his name
- receiving baptism

Thanks for joining us on this journey of exploring how God makes us new!

REFLECTION & DISCUSSION QUESTIONS

1. How does sin separate us from God?

_____

_____

_____

_____

_____

_____

_____

2. What was the purpose of the law which God gave
   the ancient Israelites?

_____

_____

_____

_____

_____

_____

_____

3. Read Romans 8:3. Why is the law alone unable to reconcile us to God?

_____

_____

_____

_____

_____

_____

_____

4. Sin cannot remain in God's presence. Why not?

_____

_____

_____

_____

_____

_____

_____

5. How do you feel about sin? Do you feel about sin the way that God feels about it?

_____

_____

_____

_____

_____

_____

6. If someone asked you why it's important to be born again, how would you answer?

_____

_____

_____

_____

_____

_____

_____

_____

2

WHAT DOES IT MEAN TO PLACE OUR FAITH IN JESUS?

Answer: Believing in Jesus means that we trust and follow him as Savior, Lord, and King in all things.

Whoever believes in the Son has eternal
life, but whoever rejects the Son will not see
life, for God's wrath remains on them.
— John 3:36

I n the Gospel of John, we learn that belief is anything but passive. Its original readers were likely Jewish Christians who had been pushed out of their Jewish communities because they believed that Jesus was the Messiah. This created among the Jewish Christians discouragement, doubt, and fear. John hoped that retelling the good news of Jesus would reassure those who were suffering and prompt to action those who were wavering.

In John 9, Jesus healed a man who was blind from birth. He put mud on his eyes, and then told him to wash at the pool of Siloam. When the Jews asked the healed man what happened to him, the man simply told the story of what Jesus had done but said he did not know who Jesus was. When the Pharisees investigated the healing later, their concern rested on the fact that Jesus had healed on the Sabbath. They called Jesus a sinner. They questioned the ability of a sinner to do miracles, and they asked the healed man about Jesus. The man replied, "He is a prophet" (John 9:17).

His growing faith led to action. When the man persisted in defending Jesus to the religious leaders, they threw him out of the synagogue. When Jesus heard this, he immediately found him again. When Jesus explained his identity to the formerly blind man, Jesus asked, "Do you believe in the Son of Man?" (John 9:35). The man responded, "Lord, I believe," and worshiped him (John 9:38). Clearly, faith in Jesus is not a passive act of our mere thinking; it involves action. Interestingly, in John's Gospel, belief is never used as a noun, but it is used nearly one hundred times as a verb.[3]

After Jesus found the man in John 9, he used blindness as a spiritual metaphor: "For judgment I have come into this world, so that the blind will see and those who see will become blind" (John 9:39). Hearing him, the Pharisees asked if they too were blind. Jesus replied, "If you were blind, you would not be guilty of sin; but now that you claim you can see, your guilt remains" (John 9:41). This is the same position we find ourselves in when we are blind to our need for a new birth. Once we come to see our need clearly, we must decide to act.

When our eyes are opened to our need for salvation in Jesus, then we are ready to place our faith in him. What does it mean to place our faith in Jesus? Believing in Jesus means that we trust and follow him as Savior, Lord, and king in all things. Listen to the recurring language in the Gospel of John, as we're invited to place our faith in Jesus:

- "For God so loved the world that he gave his one and only Son, that whoever believes in him shall not perish but have eternal life" (John 3:16).
- "Whoever believes in the Son has eternal life, but whoever rejects the Son will not see life, for God's wrath remains on them" (John 3:36).

- "The work of God is this: to believe in the one he has sent" (John 6:29).
- "I am the bread of life. Whoever comes to me will never go hungry, and whoever believes in me will never by thirsty" (John 6:35).
- "For my Father's will is that everyone who looks to the Son and believes in him shall have eternal life, and I will raise them up at the last day" (John 6:40).
- "Whoever believes in me, as Scripture has said, rivers of living water will flow from within them" (John 7:38).
- "I am the resurrection and the life. The one who believes in me will live, even though they die" (John 11:25).
- "Whoever believes in me does not believe in me only, but in the one who sent me" (John 12:44).
- "I have come into the world as a light, so that no one who believes in me should stay in darkness" (John 12:46).
- "Do not let your hearts be troubled. You believe in God; believe also in me" (John 14:1).

When we place faith in Jesus, we show faith in the truth of his ministry and claims. Those who study the Bible for the first time often have questions about the miracles of Jesus. One of the earliest steps in coming to faith is accepting his miracles. Likewise, the teachings and claims of Jesus must be accepted, which may be difficult to understand from our limited human perspective. Jesus is God's Son (Mark 1:11; 9:7), and he is the Messiah, the one chosen to save the world (John 1:34). Jesus is part of the Trinity (or Godhead), which is made up of God the Father, God the Holy Spirit, and God the Son. He is an eternal being who came to earth to identify with us and create a way to save us from our sins (Hebrews 2:14–17). On earth, he obeyed the will of God the Father (John 6:38), and his miraculous ministry was done through the power of the Holy Spirit (Matthew 12:28).

Yet we should notice that "believing in" Jesus goes beyond simply believing that Jesus did miracles or spoke true teachings. It is a choice to accept Jesus, to actively entrust oneself to God for salvation and life. This involves wholehearted trust in Jesus and a shift in allegiance to him. In *Salvation by Allegiance Alone*, Matthew Bates suggests that in the first-century context faith could be understood as "allegiance or loyalty or faithfulness."[4] He points to Jesus as the universal king and how Christians would have displayed loyalty toward him as such. This allegiance could also manifest itself as

> BELIEVING IN JESUS IS TO ACTIVELY ENTRUST ONESELF TO GOD.

obedient action, such as Christ giving up his life on the cross to bring about salvation for us.[5] Bates describes faith (*pistis*) as the framework into which the action of our ongoing allegiance is also part of our salvation.[6]

The concept that Jesus is a member of the Godhead distinguishes the Christian understanding of God from other religions. In John 10:9, Jesus says, "I am the gate; whoever enters through me will be saved." If Jesus is the gate, this means that we receive salvation by acceptance of him. This means accepting him, his teachings, and his claims. It excludes our acceptance of gods from other religions and the belief that we ultimately worship the same god. When we show faith in Jesus, we show faith *in him* as both our Lord and Savior.

WHAT IS THE CONNECTION OF FAITH TO BAPTISM?

RECALL THAT WHEN THE Holy Spirit arrived on the day of Pentecost, after Jesus had ascended into heaven, Peter preached to the gathered crowd saying, "Repent and be baptized, every one of you, in the name of Jesus Christ for the forgiveness of your sins. And you will receive the gift of the Holy Spirit" (Acts 2:38). This verse shows us that the natural response to having faith is to declare that faith in baptism. This pattern was taught to the early church, and its relevance continues for us today.

Baptism is a declaration of our faith in Jesus Christ. Because of that faith, baptism is the avenue through which we receive forgiveness of our sins. While baptism is a visible way to demonstrate our faith in Jesus and accept the gift of God's grace, it does not earn our salvation. Owen Olbricht in his book on baptism writes:

BAPTISM IS A DECLARATION OF OUR FAITH IN JESUS CHRIST.

> If baptism were a work of self-accomplishment, then it could be discounted from having anything to do with salvation and forgiveness of sins. The power to remove sins is not in the water, the action of the one doing the baptizing, or the submission of the one being baptized. Only the blood of Jesus has that power (Matthew 26:28; Hebrews 9:22).[7]

Rather salvation is given by the grace of God. Martin Luther is quoted as saying, "Your baptism is nothing less than grace clutching you by the throat: a grace-full throttling, by which your sin is submerged in order that ye may remain under grace."[8] When we are baptized, we are accepting the gift of grace and forgiveness by God. We are submitting ourselves, and our will, to God.

WHAT IS THE CONNECTION
OF FAITH TO ACTION?

WHILE RECEIVING THE GIFT of salvation is an act of grace and mercy on God's part, faith is lived out in embodied action. It involves action-oriented allegiance and faithfulness to Jesus. James 2:17 says, "Faith by itself, if it is not accompanied by action, is dead." There is a connection in the Bible between belief and action, as the Renew.org book *Faithful Faith* shows us in more detail.[9]

In Matthew 12:34–35, Jesus said that the mouth speaks of what is in the heart, and the good or bad stored up in someone will come out. It is not enough merely to do the right things, but we must have the right heart. In Matthew 15, Jesus was questioned by the Pharisees and teachers of the law about why his disciples did not ceremonially wash their hands before eating. In response, Jesus told a parable. They asked him to explain it, and he replied:

> Don't you see that whatever enters the mouth goes into the stomach and then out of the body? But the things that come out of a person's mouth come from the heart, and these defile them. For out of the heart come evil thoughts—murder, adultery, sexual immorality, theft, false testimony, slander. These are what defile a person; but eating

with unwashed hands does not defile them.
(Matthew 15:17–20)

What defiles us are our thoughts and what is in our hearts. Owen Olbricht points out the words "faith" and "belief" can be defined as "trust and reliance" and stand in contrast to "disobey," "disobedient," and "disobedience."[10] Putting one's faith in Jesus involves trusting obedience. Just "doing the right things" without involving our inner selves is not enough.

Declaring our faith in Jesus is not a way to earn our salvation, but to acknowledge our need for God's help. In John 15, we see the metaphor of the vine and the branches. In verse five Jesus said, "If you remain in me and I in you, you will bear much fruit; apart from me you can do nothing." We must never forget that our first priority is to remain connected to God, to grow in our relationship with him. Our actions should come out of the overflow of that relationship and heart-connection to God.

FAITH IS FOUNDATIONAL TO REPENTANCE, CONFESSION, AND BAPTISM

As mentioned earlier, baptism is a declaration of our faith in the work of God in the world. Colossians 2:12 says that when we are buried with Jesus in baptism, we are raised with him through our "faith in the working of God, who raised him from the dead." We acknowledge that the activity and power of God are at work in our lives, communities, and world. When we have faith in God, we look forward toward salvation at the end of time, without neglecting our role in the world until then.

When we are ready to put our faith in Jesus, we are ready to let the world know that our eyes have been opened. We repent of our sins (Chapter 3), confess Jesus as Lord (Chapter 4), and show our faith publicly through baptism (Chapter 5). As we declare our faith in Jesus, we are also showing faith in his work, his message, his miracles, and his divinity. It is Jesus and his Father's most earnest desire to save us to spend eternity with them. In fact, shortly before his death in John 17, Jesus spent a significant amount of time praying for his disciples then and today. While our faith begins on the inside, that relationship overflows into everyday life, and our faith in Jesus shines throughout the rest of our lives.

REFLECTION & DISCUSSION QUESTIONS

1. Faith in the Bible involves far more than mental assent; it involves action. What are some unfortunate consequences of having a faith that is nothing more than holding correct beliefs (and not taking action based on those beliefs)?

_____

_____

_____

_____

_____

2. Describe a time when you knew you needed to take action, but you didn't take it.

_____

_____

_____

_____

_____

_____

3. How would you explain to someone the difference between just believing stories about Jesus and accepting and trusting your life to Jesus as his disciple?

_____

_____

_____

_____

_____

_____

4. How has it been challenging for you to accept the gift of grace and forgiveness from God?

_____

_____

_____

_____

_____

_____

5. Read Matthew 12:34–35. How has submitting your heart to Jesus and his ways changed your daily actions?

_____

_____

_____

_____

_____

_____

6. Describe a time in your life when you were tempted to do something that was not permitted by God. Did you follow the leading of the Holy Spirit to make the right decision?

_____

_____

_____

_____

_____

_____

3

WHAT DOES IT MEAN TO REPENT?

Answer: Repentance means a change in heart and behavior, turning from living for ourselves to living like Jesus.

First to those in Damascus, then to those in Jerusalem and in all Judea, and then to the Gentiles, I preached that they should repent and turn to God and demonstrate their repentance by their deeds.
— Acts 26:20

---

n the first-century Jewish world, large numbers of people were drawn to the simple message of repentance. Both John the Baptist and Jesus preached, "Repent, for the kingdom of heaven has come near" (Matthew 3:2; 4:17). Mark 1:4 tells us that John "preached a baptism of repentance for the forgiveness of sins." We will focus on forgiveness in Chapter 5 of this book, but here we'll focus on repentance, pointing out the link between baptism, repentance, and forgiveness. All three of these assume humans share the same predicament: we are sinful (Romans 3:10). In fact, in order to receive forgiveness of sins, we need to confess our sins (1 John 1:9).

However, confessing one's personal sins—as distinguished from confessing Jesus as Lord—isn't the end of the journey of following Jesus. King Jesus calls us to a life of discipleship. Being a disciple means surrendering our own will and submitting to his. In biblical times, followers of Jesus were called to turn from their own sins and reject the worldliness of the predominant culture (Romans 12:2). Today we are also called to turn from our sin toward God. Repentance is a change of mind and change in action. The Greek noun used in the New Testament that we translate as "repentance" is *metanoia*. Both *metanoia* and its verb form, *metanoeō*, had been used by Greek philosophers for centuries to describe a change of mind, but by Jesus' day, the Jews also used it to refer to a change of behavior.[11] So when Peter told a crowd of onlookers to "repent and be baptized" (Acts 2:38), he was calling them to change their lives—a process that begins at baptism, yes, but continues for a lifetime (2 Corinthians 7:1). John Mark Hicks and Greg Taylor rightly describe the relationship between repentance and baptism like this:

> Baptism signals transformation, but God's work in us is far from complete. Though discipleship begins before baptism, the event of immersion marks a new identity, ethic, and world view that defines discipleship. . . . Baptism marks a lifetime process of dying to sin and renewing our appeal to God for a new life.[12]

WHAT DOES REPENTANCE LOOK LIKE?

AN EXAMPLE OF BIBLICAL repentance is found in Acts 19. The Holy Spirit had been working miracles through Paul, and after one particularly remarkable display of God's power (Acts 19:13–16), Luke describes the response of the people of Ephesus:

> When this became known to the Jews and Greeks living in Ephesus, they were all seized with fear,

and the name of the Lord Jesus was held in high honor. Many of those who believed now came and openly confessed what they had done. A number who had practiced sorcery brought their scrolls together and burned them publicly. When they calculated the value of the scrolls, the total came to fifty thousand drachmas. In this way the word of the Lord spread widely and grew in power. (Acts 19:17–20)

Here we see that repentance followed belief in the Lord Jesus, and it involved an admission of sin and a dramatic turning away from that sin—a single act that cost the equivalent of fifty thousand days' wages! But those new disciples were not merely destroying their sinful instruments; they were signifying that they were turning away from their former lifestyles, never to return again.

Yet not all repentance is demonstrated in grandiose deeds of sacrifice. When people asked John the Baptist what repentance would look like for them, he gave practical advice:

And the crowds asked him, "What then shall we do?" And he answered them, "Whoever has two tunics is to share with him who has none, and whoever has food is to do likewise." Tax collectors also came to be baptized and said to him, "Teacher, what shall we do?" And he said to them, "Collect no more than you are authorized to do." Soldiers also asked him, "And we, what shall we do?" And he said to them, "Do not extort money from anyone by threats or by false accusation, and be content with your wages." (Luke 3:10–14, ESV)

These aren't grandiose demonstrations of religious devotion—sharing your food and clothing; not abusing your position—but they are the very kinds of "mundane" acts that reflect a changed life.

WHAT IS THE NEW LIFE?

THE APOSTLE PAUL REFLECTED on his own life in his letter to the Philippians. He had excelled above his contemporaries as a Jewish leader, yet he had more to say:

But whatever were gains to me I now consider loss for the sake of Christ. What is more, I consider everything a loss because of the surpassing worth of knowing Christ Jesus my Lord, for whose sake I have lost all things. I consider them garbage, that I may gain Christ and be found in him. (Philippians 3:7–9a)

This explains how Paul become consumed with sharing the same gospel he once despised. He still believed in the same God of Abraham, Isaac, and Jacob, but he no longer allowed his own ambitions to cloud his view of Jesus. He was convinced that losing all things was worth it, just as the man who found the pearl of great price sold all he had in order to get it (Matthew 13:46). He was truly born anew into a new existence—from persecutor to persecuted.

HE WAS TRULY BORN ANEW INTO A NEW EXISTENCE.

Here we come to a major barrier for most people when they consider Christianity: the cost that must be paid in giving up sinful behavior.[13] A story important enough to be repeated in three Gospels is that of the rich young ruler who asked Jesus how to have eternal life (Matthew 19:16–22; Mark 10:17–27; Luke 18:18–23). Jesus responded by telling him to keep God's commands. The young man explained that he had spent his life doing just that. Notice Jesus' response:

> When Jesus heard this, he said to him, "You still lack one thing. Sell everything you have and give to the poor, and you will have treasure in heaven. Then come, follow me." When he heard this, he became very sad, because he was very wealthy." (Luke 18:22–23)

Why did he go away sad? It's because the word "give" echoed so loudly in his mind that he failed to hear the words "Follow me!" He might have heard the words, but he didn't believe that they would lead to eternal life. To put it plainly, repentance is hard.

As Christians grow in their faith, we will no doubt find new areas to devote to God, and thus continue to offer ourselves a living sacrifice (Romans 12:1). We are not, however, left to make these changes on our own. The Scriptures assure us that the Holy Spirit empowers all disciples of Jesus to live holy lives and to make the sometimes difficult sacrifices that repentance requires (Romans 8:11). Some people, both inside and outside the church, think that followers of Jesus are self-righteous, but the Bible expresses a very different idea. As New Testament scholar Scot McKnight notes:

> Repentance . . . cannot be manufactured by strenuous effort. Furthermore, as the rebellious son learned, it involves both the inner and outer dimensions of life (Luke 15:14–21; cf. 2 Corinthians 7:9–10). It is a work in the heart by the Spirit of God as one is awakened to the goodness, mercy, and holiness of God.[14]

God grants repentance and provides the strength and grace for us to pursue holy lives (2 Timothy 2:25).

We are called to holiness in our private lives and in our relationships (Hebrews 12:14), but without the intervention of God, we would be powerless to achieve it. The church is, then, a fellowship of repenters. The Holy Spirit uses repentance to build a holy community of believers as we forgive and receive forgiveness. In fact, when true repentance takes place, a beautiful fellowship of grace is offered and received.[15] While it is not the purpose of this book to explore the fullness of God's eternal design for the church, we must understand that a lifelong habit of repentance is impossible without a loving community of support.

Ancient Christians knew this, so they frequently pointed to repentance as an act of love. For example, one of the earliest ancient Christian documents records:

> Therefore let us love one another, so that we all may enter into the kingdom of God. While we still have time to be healed, let us place ourselves in the hands of God the physician, and pay him what is due. What is that? Sincere, heartfelt repentance.[16]

As you travel the path of repentance, God is calling you to show love to those whom you have wronged or neglected. Repentance can be demonstrated by a long talk, a gracious letter, or a humble act of service to a former enemy. We must demonstrate repentance in how we treat our friends and those most difficult to love.

One last word on repentance is appropriate. Many in the world think that repentance means turning to a dry, stale religious life. However, the Gospels say just the opposite. Luke records several stories of repentance involving feasts, which make clear that the best life comes from repentance. Levi, also known as Matthew, was the tax collector who left his profession and immediately threw a banquet for Jesus and his former associates. When the prodigal son repented, his father hosted a huge celebration. The son had left home to find joy, but instead wound up in a pig pen. His path to true happiness involved coming back to his father—and joining in on the celebration! The tagline of the previous parables in Luke 15 is, "In the same way, I tell you, there is rejoicing in the presence of the angels of God over one sinner who repents" (15:10; cf. Luke 15:7). Likewise, the story of Zacchaeus reminds us that when a sinner meets Jesus (and later feasts with him), they experience the joy of repentance: "Here and now I give half of my possessions to the poor, and if I have cheated anybody out of anything, I will pay back four times the amount" (Luke 19:8). When a person becomes a disciple of Jesus, they are born again. Their life begins again. From then on, their journey will be shaped by the Lord's and not their own will. This is biblical repentance.

REFLECTION & DISCUSSION QUESTIONS

1. What is the connection between confession and repentance?

_____

_____

_____

_____

_____

_____

2. If someone asked you what makes repentance important, how would you answer?

_____

_____

_____

_____

_____

_____

_____

3. When has God convicted you of a specific sin? How did you turn from it?

_____

_____

_____

_____

_____

_____

_____

4. Describe what new life looked like for Paul in Philippians 3:7–9. What are some specific ways he changed?

_____

_____

_____

_____

_____

_____

_____

5. How we live our lives is the best example of our repentant hearts. What do people see in your life that demonstrates a repentant heart?

_____

_____

_____

_____

_____

_____

6. How can you develop a life of regular confession and repentance?

_____

_____

_____

_____

_____

_____

_____

4

WHAT DOES IT MEAN TO CONFESS JESUS AS LORD?

Answer: Confession of Jesus as Lord is a declaration of allegiance to Jesus as king and a rejection of all other claims of lordship.

And now what are you waiting for?
Get up, be baptized and wash your
sins away, calling on his name.
— Acts 22:16

When you read the book of Acts, you may notice that there is no simple list of steps for someone to become a disciple of Jesus. For example, as quoted earlier, Peter commanded the crowd in Jerusalem, "Repent and be baptized, every one of you, in the name of Jesus Christ for the forgiveness of your sins. And you will receive the gift of the Holy Spirit" (Acts 2:38). In Acts 8, some Samaritans "accepted the word of God" (8:14), were baptized, and then received the Holy Spirit (8:16–17). In that same chapter, the Ethiopian eunuch learned the gospel from Philip and was baptized (Acts 8:26–40). Paul's conversion is told three times in Acts—Acts 9; Acts 22; Acts 26—and in each story, he mentioned different elements of his salvation. According to Acts 9:18, after Paul's encounter with Jesus, he was baptized, and we find out later why. He was told, "Get up, be baptized and wash your sins away, calling on his name" (Acts 22:16). In Acts 26, Paul mentioned nothing of his baptism.

This brief survey of a few narratives in Acts demonstrates the common figure of speech known as metonymy, wherein one part of a concept embodies the entire thing. The New Testament uses metonymy to describe what it means to become a Christian. We see these truths in the New Testament:

- To be a follower of Jesus means that you believe in him.
- To be baptized means you are a believer.
- To be a believer means that you have confessed Jesus as your Lord.
- To have confessed Jesus as Lord means you have repented of your sins.
- To have repented of your sins means that you have received the Holy Spirit.

Any of these terms can be a metonymy describing the entire process, which begins at the new birth. So Paul can say in Romans 10:10, "For it is with your heart that you believe and are justified, and it is with your mouth that you profess your faith and are saved." Belief and confession are necessary parts of the process, but that doesn't mean repentance and baptism are excluded. Instead, the new birth begins when a person no longer claims their own lordship, but instead surrenders to King Jesus. Hearing, believing, repenting, confessing, being baptized, and receiving the Spirit are all crucial elements of the new birth.

WHAT IS THE "GOOD CONFESSION"?

UNFORTUNATELY, THROUGHOUT HISTORY THE church has tended to emphasize certain elements of the new birth and neglect others. When the church began baptizing infants in the third century, the role faith plays in discipleship was muddied. When penance—an outward demonstration of repentance such as saying a required number of prayers—was emphasized, the importance of the Holy Spirit was often ignored. When the Reformers attempted to correct these omissions by placing greater emphasis on faith (*sola fide*, "by faith alone") and grace (*sola gratia*, "by grace alone"), they offered a helpful corrective, but they also tended to neglect the important role that repentance and baptism play in the new birth. As the renowned Reformed theologian Karl Barth remarked:

> It is a strange gap in the baptismal teaching, of all Confessions—the Reformed included—that the meaning and work of baptism have never been understood in principle as a glorifying of God, that is as a moment in his self-revelation.[17]

Protestants have unfortunately tended to de-emphasize baptism because they feared the focus on what humans do, not on the God-glorifying moment when Jesus shines through the newly baptized person.

Following this idea, confessing Jesus is not a mere religious rite. It is a moment of cognitive and verbal affirmation, publicly proclaiming that Jesus is Lord and Christ, and it is the beginning of the process of a lifelong commitment.[18] Paul admonished Timothy, "Take hold of the eternal life to which you were called when you made your *good confession* in the presence of many witnesses" (1 Timothy 6:12b). In fact, Jesus also made the good confession (Matthew 27:11; Mark 15:2; Luke 23:3), as did Peter (Matthew 16:16; Mark 8:29; Luke 9:20). In addition, Jesus emphasized that his disciples needed to be willing to make the good confession in the face of a hostile world at any time:

> Therefore, everyone who confesses Me before people, I will also confess him before My Father who is in heaven. But whoever denies Me before people, I will also deny him before My Father who is in heaven. (Matthew 10:32–33, NASB)

Jesus knew that his first followers would face pressure from family and friends to shy away from their faith in him, and he directly challenged them to openly confess their devotion to him.

WHY DO WE CONFESS JESUS AS MESSIAH AND LORD?

WE CALL THE "GOOD confession" what Christians confess out loud when they convert to Christ. Early Christian formulations of the good confession point to two important ideas. First, confessing that Jesus is the "Christ" is saying that he is the promised Messiah of Israel. The Old Testament contains promises, titles, prophecies, and sufferings regarding the Messiah, and Jesus fulfilled them all. Second, confessing Jesus is Lord acknowledges him as God and king of the universe—and, therefore, king over our lives. That's why Peter preached in his first gospel sermon, "Therefore let all Israel be assured of this: God has made this Jesus, whom you crucified, both *Lord* and *Messiah*" (Acts 2:36).

One of the earliest formulations of the good confession is found in Acts 8:37, where an Ethiopian official heard and believed the gospel. The story describes his baptism and belief. But what did he believe? The earliest Greek manuscripts do not tell us, but later manuscripts do. The King James Version documents the eunuch's statement: "I believe that Jesus Christ is the Son of God" (Acts 8:37). Whether this reflects the actual statement made by the eunuch on that day, or it is an insertion made by an early Christian scribe, it nevertheless reflects an early Christian version of the good confession. In the Roman world, to say Jesus was the "Son of God" was to say that he was Lord and King.[19]

Just how significant was it at the time to confess Jesus as Lord, especially when "lord" had more than one meaning at the time? Today, most modern English-speaking countries don't regularly use the word "lord." Mostly, it is used in Britain and its commonwealth countries to refer to someone with a political role, or it is used as a religious word. We can see this broader usage of the word "lord" (*kurios* in Greek) in England's 1611 King James Version of the Bible. For example, in Matthew 10:24, while the NIV says, "The student is not above the teacher, nor a servant above his master," the KJV has, "The disciple is not above his master, nor the servant above his lord." In Greek, terms such as *kurios* reflected a difference in social or religious status.[20] A Greek-speaking Jew in the first-century Roman world could gladly say that Jehovah God is the Lord and still refer to his social superior (master, government official, royalty) as lord.[21]

However, there were times when followers of God had to make it clear that they would worship Jehovah God alone. To understand the implications of confessing Jesus as Lord, we must place this confession against the backdrop of the Roman Empire. When Jesus was born, there was already a powerful king who called himself "Son of God." It was Augustus Caesar.[22] While he did not envision himself as the Jewish messiah, he did claim for himself the right to absolute obedience from his subjects. Augustus also began a tradition of Roman emperors who called themselves "Father of the fatherland." They envisioned their empire to be one big family of which they were head, appointed by the gods to offer blessings and discipline to their children.

The average pagan Roman of the time would have no problem recognizing his social superior as lord, as well as the emperor himself. This is why modern Christian historians such as N. T. Wright have pointed out that when believers claimed Jesus as Lord in the early church, they weren't simply making a personal religious commitment. They were rejecting all earthly claimants to ultimate allegiance—familial, political, and social—in favor of Jesus. To say Jesus was Lord was to say Caesar was not.[23] This does not mean that the early Christians saw themselves as revolutionaries seeking to overthrow the emperor. It does mean, however, that they had to make it clear where their allegiances lay. This is the point of making the good confession.

An important early Christian document from the second century called *The Martyrdom of Polycarp* recounts the story of the aged Christian leader Polycarp. He was being led to his death for his Christian faith, when some attempted to get him to try and save himself by simply swearing allegiance to Caesar and the Roman gods. The author explains:

> They also, transferring him to their carriage, were trying to persuade him, sitting beside him and

saying, "For what harm is it to say 'Caesar is Lord' and to offer incense," and so forth, and thus to be delivered. And he did not answer them at first. But, as they were persisting, he said, "I am not about to do what you are advising me."[24]

Why would this old man refuse to save his life with a simple statement that Caesar was *kurios*? As he was about to die, Polycarp explained, "For eighty-six years I have been serving him, and he has done me no wrong. How then can I blaspheme my King who has saved me?"[25]

DO WE CONFESS ALONE?

To CONFESS JESUS AS Lord means that we make a public proclamation that we are submitting our lives to him alone. Even if others refuse to join us, we realize we each must stand before the Lord to be judged as individuals. However, confession is not a solo endeavor. In fact, believers need to come together regularly to confess Jesus as Lord to encourage and remind each other of their king and his kingdom.

BELIEVERS NEED TO REMIND EACH OTHER OF THEIR KING AND HIS KINGDOM.

Throughout the centuries, Jewish synagogues have collectively recited an important confession from Scripture they call the *Shema*, which means "to hear" in Hebrew. It is called by this name because of the first word of the proclamation, which is found in Deuteronomy 6:4, "Hear [*shema*], O Israel: The LORD our God, the LORD is one." Since the very first Christians were all Jewish, they continued to share this firm belief in the one God of Israel, but they added an important element to the confession in the *Shema*. Paul wrote to the Corinthians:

> For us there is but one God, the Father, from whom all things came and for whom we live; and there is but one Lord, Jesus Christ, through whom all things came and through whom we live. (1 Corinthians 8:6)

Many biblical scholars believe that Paul was quoting one of the earliest Christian confessions, which added the lordship of Jesus to the oneness of God. In the context of 1 Corinthians 8, he used it to admonish Christians to look out for one another and refrain from causing another believer to sin. There are scores of these early Christian confessions embedded in the New Testament. For example, Paul wrote to Timothy, "For there is one God and one mediator between God and mankind, the man Christ Jesus, who gave himself as a ransom for all people" (1 Timothy 2:5–6a).

As Christianity spread throughout the Roman Empire and beyond, the gospel message left its original Jewish context and entered into a pagan matrix that accepted many competing gods. Christians continued to formulate confessions of Jesus' lordship to help explain who Jesus was in a polytheistic culture, and these confessions eventually came together to form the great creeds of Christianity.

The word "creed" comes from the Latin for *credo*, which means "I believe." Creeds are merely statements of belief, and in the first centuries of the Christian church, they helped bind believers in a unified confession of Jesus' lordship. One of the earliest creeds was recorded by the church father Justin Martyr in the middle of the second century. It states:

> We piously believe in the God of the Christians, whom we regard to be the only one of these things from the beginning, the Maker and Fashioner of the whole creation, what is visible and invisible; and the Lord Jesus Christ, Child of God, who was proclaimed beforehand by the prophets as one who was going to be present with the race of humanity, the herald of salvation and teacher of good doctrines.[26]

Perhaps you have heard of the famous creeds from later centuries, such as the Nicene Creed or the Apostles' Creed. While they are not Scripture and should not be considered divinely inspired, they demonstrate how important it has always been for Christians to be ready to confess Jesus as Lord, both to each other and to the world. In a culture noisy with competing calls for our allegiance, we believers in Jesus continue to confess that he is Lord. In this way, we encourage faithfulness in each other and reaffirm our reason for confidence.

REFLECTION & DISCUSSION QUESTIONS

1. What are some of the components of the salvation process that are used in the book of Acts to represent the entire process (what this chapter refers to as metonymy)?

2. If someone asked you why they should confess Jesus as Lord before people and not just privately, how would you answer?

3. Give specific reasons to declare that Jesus is both Christ and Lord.

_____

_____

_____

_____

_____

_____

_____

_____

4. What are some practical examples of how you have submitted your life to Jesus' care and control?

_____

_____

_____

_____

_____

_____

_____

5. Why is it important to confess Jesus as Lord regularly in a Christian community?

_____

_____

_____

_____

_____

_____

_____

6. As you've matured in your Christian faith, how has the significance of declaring your allegiance to Jesus changed?

_____

_____

_____

_____

_____

_____

_____

_____

5

WHAT DOES IT MEAN TO BE BAPTIZED FOR THE FORGIVENESS OF OUR SINS?

Answer: Baptism is the normative place where our faith connects with God's grace and we become new, with a clean slate and a restored relationship with God.

Peter replied, "Repent and be baptized, every one of you, in the name of Jesus Christ for the forgiveness of your sins. And you will receive the gift of the Holy Spirit."
— Acts 2:38

After God created the earth, he called it "good." But it didn't take long for Adam and Eve to sin. In fact, they sinned even before the second generation began. Genesis 3:8 tells us they heard God walking in the garden and hid themselves. The narrative implies that Adam and Eve were familiar with God through these sorts of walks. It appears that God enjoyed fellowship with Adam and Eve in the Garden of Eden. Imagine that: being able to converse with God, asking questions and receiving answers much like you would with a friend!

Sin entered the world and created an issue for all humanity because it destroyed our once close relationship with God by creating a separation between us and God.[27] We are called to be holy because God is holy. Leviticus 11:44 says, "I am the LORD your God; consecrate yourselves and be holy, because I am holy." We are to strive for holiness in order to be in God's presence, knowing that ultimately our humanity will get in the way despite our best efforts. Like Adam and Eve we have all sinned and fallen short of God's glory (Romans 3:23), and our sin separates us from God. Isaiah 59:1–2 addresses this issue:

> Surely the arm of the LORD is not too short to save,
> nor his ear too dull to hear.

> But your iniquities have separated
> you from your God;
> Your sins have hidden his face from you,
> so that he will not hear.

While this passage from Isaiah notes the separation that sin creates between us and God, it also bears good news: the Lord can save us.

WHAT IS THE CONNECTION OF OUR BAPTISM TO JESUS' BAPTISM?

WHEN JESUS WENT TO John the Baptist to be baptized, John initially resisted, saying, "I need to be baptized by you, and do you come to me?" (Matthew 3:14). But Jesus replied, "Let it be so now; it is proper for us to do this to fulfill all righteousness" (Matthew 3:15). So John baptized Jesus. By being baptized, Jesus set an example for us to follow. By undergoing baptism, Christ identified with broken humanity. As Vander Zee says,

> Jesus, being the sinless one, did not have to repent of sin, but he nevertheless buried himself in the waters of repentance with sinners. In his baptism, Jesus identifies himself as our brother and there begins to assume our sin and guilt.[28]

While Jesus didn't need forgiveness, we do, and we claim that forgiveness at our baptism. When we are baptized, Colossians 2:12 says, we are "buried with him in baptism" and "raised with him through [our] faith." Our baptism symbolizes Jesus' ultimate sacrifice for our sins and his resurrection into newness of life. Romans 6:4–5 says this:

> We were therefore buried with him through baptism into death in order that, just as Christ was raised from the dead through the glory of the Father, we too may live a new life. For if we have been united with him in a death like his, we will certainly also be united with him in a resurrection like his.

This promise of new life with Christ is a beautiful gift from God. A chance to start again, and to make things right with God. A chance to spend eternity with God forever.

WHY DO WE NEED TO HAVE OUR SINS "WASHED AWAY"?

IN THE WATER OF baptism, our sins are washed away. This teaching is made explicit in Acts 22:16 and the Nicene Creed, which ends with the expression, "We acknowledge one baptism unto remission of sins."[29] Another word for sin is "transgression." In Colossians 2:13, Paul says those who were once dead in their transgressions are now "alive together with Him, having forgiven us all our wrongdoings" (NASB). G. Walter Hansen says in his commentary on Galatians:

> A transgression is the violation of a standard. The law provides the objective standard by which the violations are measured. In order for sinners to know how sinful they really are, how far they deviate from God's standards, God gave the law. Before the law was given, there was sin (see Rom 5:13). But after the law was given, sin could be clearly specified and measured (see Rom 3:20; 4:15; 7:7).[30]

God's law provided a standard by which sin could be recognized. God's standards, as recorded in his Word, are the measurement by which we should base our lives. When we sin, we violate God's standard, causing a rift in our relationship with him. God's desire for relationship with his people was steadfast, even though the people fell short. He wanted to maintain the relationship and forgive their sins. In Jeremiah 33:8, God looked forward to forgiving Israel. He said, "I will cleanse them from all the sin they have committed against me and will forgive their sins of rebellion against me." We see this desire to have relationship with people from the Garden of Eden in Genesis to the Tree of Life in Revelation. In Scriptures such as Jeremiah 33:8, we can see God's desire to have a relationship with people. At times in wisdom literature and the prophets, he seems to ache for a renewed relationship with his people.

WHAT DOES JESUS PROVIDE THAT THE LAW CANNOT?

IN THE OLD TESTAMENT, God provided a means to restore relationship through the giving of the law. The law's purpose was to train the Israelites about what was right and wrong. This was important because when they left Egypt, they were beaten down and struggled with their identity as the people of God. God had to train them how to be holy and follow his ways.

When I teach class, I (Anessa) compare the purpose of the law to bowling alley bumpers, which are used for children's birthday parties. The bumpers increase the chance of hitting the mark, and they help young bowlers develop some skills along the way. In the same way, the law helped the Israelites follow the law carefully, so they would have some success in holiness. At first, this required merely doing what they were told to do. But the real goal was for God's law to seep deeply into their character and change their heart. Deuteronomy 6:5 instructed Israel to love God with their heart and soul.

However, as mentioned earlier, the law was inadequate to bridge the rift completely. God promised a Messiah to save Israel, and then he sent his Son, Jesus, to fulfill the law and be the ultimate sacrifice (1 John 4:9; Hebrews 10:12). The purpose of these actions was to save us from our sins by forgiving us. The Greek word for "save" is *sōzō*. It also means to "deliver," "protect," "heal," "preserve," and "make whole."[31] Baptism plays a role in restoring our relationship with God by removing our sins and healing our relationship with him. This was something that the law was incapable of doing on its own, and it required Jesus to be the final sacrifice in order to restore our relationship with God.

WHAT IS THE CONNECTION OF BAPTISM TO FORGIVENESS?

THE NEW TESTAMENT MAKES frequent connections between baptism and forgiveness. For example, Ananias—who would soon baptize Paul—told him, "Get up, be baptized and wash your sins away, calling on his name" (Acts 22:16). Peter told the crowd at Pentecost, "Repent and be baptized, every one of you, in the name of Jesus Christ for the forgiveness of your sins. And you will receive the gift of the Holy Spirit"

(Acts 2:38). When we are raised from the water of baptism, we are new people with new, clean slates. The Greek verb "to forgive" is *aphiēmi*. It connotes "sending away," which is exactly what happens in the water of baptism: baptism sends our sins away from us.[32] God himself sanctifies us and gives us forgiveness of our sins (Acts 26:18).

Baptism is the normative time at which we are forgiven of our sins and are given the Holy Spirit (Acts 2:38). However, it is also worth noting that in Acts we see that God can sovereignly choose to give the Spirit before baptism (e.g., Cornelius in Acts 10:44–48) and after baptism (e.g., the Samaritans in Acts 8:12–18). We know that God looks at the heart in conversion (Acts 15:8–9), not just our actions. So we want to make sure we uphold this norm without limiting our understanding of God's sovereign role in granting salvation. The Roman Catholic Church has a saying, "God has bound salvation to the sacrament of Baptism, but he himself is not bound by his sacraments."[33]

HOW SHOULD WE BE BAPTIZED?

OVER THE PAST TWO thousand years, adopting human theology rather than Jesus' teachings created confusion about how one should be baptized. The baptisms of John the Baptist, Jesus, and the disciples all demonstrate baptism by immersion. In fact, the Greek word for "baptism" is *baptizō*, which means "to dip" or "to immerse."[34] During the second century, the practice of baptism developed consistency. The early church practiced immersion, except for one example in the *Didache* when enough water was not present. That was referred to as the act of "pouring" rather than baptism.[35] John Mark Hicks and Greg Taylor write about this adaptation, saying:

> This diversity, while minor at first, grew through the fifth century and by the end of the medieval period a consensus had been established that was the opposite of the practice of the second-century church. . . . However, one constant was a consensus understanding that baptism was for the remission of sins and that an unbaptized saved adult was a rare exception.[36]

By journeying back and reading baptism stories in the Scriptures and examining the original Greek word for "baptism," we discover immersion as the normative mode of baptism envisioned in the New Testament. By participating in this act, we are weaving our own story into the tapestry of Christ and of Christians throughout the world spanning across two millennia.

AFTER WE'RE FORGIVEN, WHAT'S NEXT?

FORGIVENESS GIVES US A clean slate, one that must be filled with God. While forgiveness happens at once, the lifelong process of pursuing holiness begins. Theologian Stanley Grenz writes:

> When seen from our vantage point, therefore, the experience of salvation occurs in three stages. "Conversion" marks the inauguration of personal salvation. The transformation the Spirit effects in us is a lifelong process which we label "sanctification." We anticipate at the end of the age our "glorification," the completion of the Spirit's work of renewal.[37]

In 2 Thessalonians 2:13, we learn that we are "saved through the sanctifying work of the Spirit and through belief in the truth." While it is God who sanctifies us, we are also expected to pursue purity. The good news is that God wants us to succeed in this. In fact, Jesus prayed for the sanctification of his present and future disciples before his crucifixion: "My prayer is not for them alone. I pray also for those who will believe in me through their message" (John 17:20). This is an important process because those

GOD WANTS US TO SUCCEED IN THIS.

who are sanctified are given an inheritance in him (Acts 20:32). The Holy Spirit was given to us to help us. God wants us to succeed!

Our first step in joining God in the process is our baptism, as we've mentioned, where we are buried and resurrected *with Jesus.* Being baptized does not mean a life without temptation or struggle. As forgiven people whom Jesus is sanctifying, we must invest ourselves into the process of sanctification, not cheapening the incredible sacrifice of Christ in forgiving our sins by not pursuing holiness. Owen Olbricht explains the importance of our personal investment well:

> In order for baptism to be valid, the one submitting to the physical act must also be spiritually involved. He must understand that he is being forgiven of past sins. He must understand that his burial and resurrection ends an old life—that he is entering into a new relationship with Jesus and is accepting his lordship.[38]

When we remove sin from our lives, it leaves a void to be filled. If we do not intentionally fill that void with righteousness, sin creeps back in. We remember this ourselves, and when we disciple others, we need to be prepared to walk with them through spiritual struggles into holiness.

AM I READY TO GET BAPTIZED?

ONE QUESTION THAT OFTEN comes up when someone is studying to become a Christian is if a person is ready to take the step of baptism. The one considering baptism often feels pressure to have it all together and have all their questions answered before taking this step. However, if we look at the ministry of Jesus, we see examples of the apostles teaching, followed by people immediately responding in baptism (Acts 2:38–41; Acts 10:47–48; Acts 16:32–33; Acts 19:4–5). The urgency of their decision surely indicated that they did not have every question answered, but that they understood their need for a Savior. Part of growing a deeper faith is asking questions, and this is also a sign of our humanity.

One example of a believer's questioning is John the Baptist in Luke 7:18–23. John the Baptist faithfully lived out his role as the forerunner to the Messiah and even baptized Jesus. However, while he was in prison, he began to question whether Jesus was truly the Messiah. John sent his followers to ask Jesus if he was the one they were expecting or if there would be another. This brings comfort, because if John the Baptist can ask tough questions, it is reasonable to expect that we may too. Any unrealistic expectation that all our questions must be answered before we get baptized could keep us from taking this step.

The gift of the Spirit helps us with our spiritual walk and can help us find answers to our questions. Even if we are stuck with a particular faith question for an extended period before baptism, but decide to move ahead with repentance and baptism, we can end up figuring out the answer to our questions post-baptism. This displays how the Spirit reveals Jesus' message and guides people to truth after immersion (John 16:12–15; Romans 8:1–17). He also helps us overcome sin once we've been born again (Romans 8:13–14; Galatians 5:24). The Holy Spirit is a powerful resource we are granted access to at baptism. Again, that God gives us this gift shows us that he wants us to succeed.

Part of having faith is taking the step and trusting God to provide what we need. I (Anessa) remember having a conversation about the Christian life with a woman I had great respect for in college. She was married to a prominent leader in the school and in the church, and she was nearing retirement age. She told me that someday she hoped to have "this Christianity thing all worked out." I felt immediately reassured that I did not have to have it all together, and then a little fear. Was it ever possible to "make it" in our Christian walk?

I have discovered that the Christian life is a journey. If we wait to act until we are perfect or have it all together, then we will be waiting forever. God accepts us as we are when we take the step of baptism, and he walks with us as we grow. We must take that step of faith in faith.

A COMMITMENT TO BE A DISCIPLE OF JESUS

BAPTISM IS NOT THE finish line, but the starting line. Baptism expresses our commitment to discipleship. A disciple is someone who is following Jesus, being changed by Jesus, and is committed to the mission of Jesus (Matthew 4:19). The focus of our lives is not just on eternity but also on life in God's kingdom, here and now. We want to live our lives as Jesus would if he were living our lives in our bodies.

The apostle Paul poignantly describes something similar, focusing on his post-conversion life as a disciple:

> I have been crucified with Christ and I no longer live, but Christ lives in me. The life I live in the body, I live by faith in the Son of God, who loved me and gave himself for me. (Galatians 2:20)

> I eagerly expect and hope that I will in no way be ashamed, but will have sufficient courage so that now as always Christ will be exalted in my body, whether by life or by death. For to me, to live is Christ and to die is gain. (Philippians 1:20–21)

But whatever were gains to me I now consider loss for the sake of Christ. What is more, I consider everything a loss because of the surpassing worth of knowing Christ Jesus my Lord. . . . I want to know Christ—yes, to know the power of his resurrection and participation in his sufferings, becoming like him in his death. (Philippians 3:7–10)

Like Paul, we want Christ to live in us, to see him exalted in our bodies, and even to share in his sufferings, if needed. After baptism, as spiritual infants, we come up and out of the waters to live for Jesus. In the light of this vision for living like Jesus, Paul describes our post-baptism life as a brand-new life (Romans 6:4).

And just like spiritual infants need a parent to guide them and raise them, when we rise from the waters of baptism, we need mature disciples to teach us how to live as disciples of Jesus. In this way, we learn how to live our lives as disciples who recognize the incredible gift of forgiveness we have been granted and the vitally important life to which God has called us, both here and now in this world and then and there in the afterlife.

WE NEED MATURE DISCIPLES TO TEACH US HOW TO LIVE AS DISCIPLES OF JESUS.

REFLECTION & DISCUSSION QUESTIONS

1. If someone asked you what baptism is, how would you answer?

_____

_____

_____

_____

_____

_____

2. Paraphrase Romans 6:3–6 in your own words.

_____

_____

_____

_____

_____

_____

3. How do we know God's standards for our lives?

_____

_____

_____

_____

_____

_____

_____

4. How does baptism restore our relationship
   with God?

_____

_____

_____

_____

_____

_____

_____

5. Describe how the Holy Spirit helps you live a God-centered life.

_____

_____

_____

_____

_____

_____

_____

6. What are some examples of the sanctification process in your own life?

_____

_____

_____

_____

_____

_____

_____

CONCLUSION

*Our entire spiritual life is the activation
of the seed planted in baptism.*
— Mark the Ascetic (sixth century)[39]

I n the five brief chapters of this book, we have attempted to demonstrate the importance of the new birth
into Jesus Christ. While there's always more to say, we
believe that the message of the new birth is actually simple: we all need to be born again into the kingdom of
God. The emphasis is not on
the good that we do in the
flesh (though good deeds will
surely follow), but on the work
that God begins in us through

**WE ALL NEED
TO BE BORN
AGAIN INTO THE
KINGDOM OF GOD.**

the Spirit. Paul wrote that God "saved us, not because of
righteous things we had done, but because of his mercy.
He saved us through the washing of rebirth and renewal
by the Holy Spirit" (Titus 3:5).

Just as it was good news in biblical times to hear that Jesus offers people a new life, so it is good news today. Rebirth. Renewal. Resurrection. God can take his creation, though seemingly dead, and make it new again. This is the divine miracle we were created for. Our individual stories join up with Jesus' story when he begins to breathe new life into them. C. S. Lewis observed, "Death and resurrection are what the story is about and had we but eyes to see it, this has been hinted on every page, met us, in some disguise, at every turn."[40]

John writes, "Unless a kernel of wheat falls to the ground and dies, it remains only a single seed. But if it dies, it produces many seeds" (John 12:24). The world says that we are born, we live, and we die. But Jesus says, *You can be born again into a life with meaning and hope.* We pray that you find life in Jesus and that you plant the seeds of new birth into the hearts of a dying world.

APPENDIX A

BOOK RECOMMENDATIONS
FOR FURTHER STUDY

Rees Bryant, *Baptism, Why Wait?: Faith's Response in Conversion* (Joplin: College Press, 1999).

Jack Cottrell, *Baptism: A Biblical Study* (Joplin: College Press, 2006).

Everett Ferguson, *Baptism in the Early Church: History, Theology, and Liturgy in the First Five Centuries* (Grand Rapids: Eerdmans, 2009).

John Mark Hicks and Greg Taylor, *Down in the River to Pray: Revisioning Baptism as God's Transforming Work* (Siloam Springs, AR: Leafwood Publishers, 2004).

Tony Twist, Bobby Harrington, and David Young, *Baptism: What the Bible Teaches* (Renew.org, 2019).

APPENDIX B

RENEW.ORG NETWORK LEADERS' VALUES AND FAITH STATEMENTS

Mission: We Renew the Teachings of
Jesus to Fuel Disciple Making

Vision: A collaborative network equipping
millions of disciples, disciple makers, and
church planters among all ethnicities.

SEVEN VALUES

RENEWAL IN THE BIBLE and in history follows a discernible outline that can be summarized by seven key elements. We champion these elements as our core values. They are listed in a sequential pattern that is typical of renewal, and it all starts with God.

1. *Renewing by God's Spirit.* We believe that God is the author of renewal and that he invites us to access and join him through prayer and fasting for the Holy Spirit's work of renewal.

2. *Following God's Word.* We learn the ways of God with lasting clarity and conviction by trusting God's Word and what it teaches as the objective foundation for renewal and life.

3. *Surrendering to Jesus' Lordship.* The gospel teaches us that Jesus is Messiah (King) and Lord. He calls everyone to salvation (in eternity) and discipleship (in this life) through a faith commitment that is expressed in repentance, confession, and baptism. Repentance and surrender to Jesus as Lord is the never-ending cycle for life in Jesus' kingdom, and it is empowered by the Spirit.

4. *Championing disciple making.* Jesus personally gave us his model of disciple making, which he demonstrated with his disciples. Those same principles from the life of Jesus should be utilized as we make disciples today and champion discipleship as the core mission of the local church.

5. *Loving like Jesus.* Jesus showed us the true meaning of love and taught us that sacrificial love is the

distinguishing character trait of true disciples (and true renewal). Sacrificial love is the foundation for our relationships both in the church and in the world.

6. *Living in holiness.* Just as Jesus lived differently from the world, the people in his church will learn to live differently than the world. Even when it is difficult, we show that God's kingdom is an alternative kingdom to the world.

7. *Leading courageously.* God always uses leaders in renewal who live by a prayerful, risk-taking faith. Renewal will be led by bold and courageous leaders—who make disciples, plant churches, and create disciple making movements.

TEN FAITH STATEMENTS

WE BELIEVE THAT JESUS Christ is Lord. We are a group of church leaders inviting others to join the theological and disciple making journey described below. We want to trust and follow Jesus Christ to the glory of God the Father in the power of the Holy Spirit. We are committed to *restoring* the kingdom vision of Jesus and the apostles, especially the *message* of Jesus' gospel, the *method* of disciple making he showed us, and the *model* of what a community of his disciples, at their best, can become.

We live in a time when cultural pressures are forcing us to face numerous difficulties and complexities in following God. Many are losing their resolve. We trust that God is gracious and forgives the errors of those with genuine faith in his Son, but our desire is to be faithful in all things.

Our focus is disciple making, which is both reaching lost people (evangelism) and bringing people to maturity (sanctification). We seek to be a movement of disciple making leaders who make disciples and other disciple makers. We want to renew existing churches and help plant multiplying churches.

1. *God's Word.* We believe God gave us the sixty-six books of the Bible to be received as the inspired, authoritative, and infallible Word of God for salvation and life. The documents of Scripture come to us as diverse literary and historical writings. Despite their complexities, they can be understood, trusted, and followed. We want to do the hard work of wrestling to understand Scripture in order to obey God. We want to avoid the errors of interpreting Scripture through the sentimental lens of our feelings and opinions or through a complex re-interpretation of plain meanings so that the Bible says what our culture says. Ours is a time for both clear thinking and courage. Because the Holy Spirit inspired all sixty-six books, we honor Jesus' Lordship by submitting our lives to all that God has for us in them.

Psalm 1; 119; Deuteronomy 4:1–6; 6:1–9;
2 Chronicles 34; Nehemiah 8; Matthew 5:1–7:28;
15:6–9; John 12:44–50; Matthew 28:19; Acts 2:42;
17:10–11; 2 Timothy 3:16–4:4; 1 Peter 1:20–21.

2. *Christian convictions.* We believe the Scriptures reveal three distinct elements of the faith: *essential* elements which are necessary for salvation; *important* elements which are to be pursued so that we faithfully follow Christ; and *personal* elements or opinion. The gospel is *essential.* Every person who is indwelt and sealed by God's Holy Spirit because of their faith in the gospel is a brother or a sister in Christ. *Important* but secondary elements of the faith are vital. Our faithfulness to God requires us to seek and pursue them, even as we acknowledge that our salvation may not be dependent on getting them right. And thirdly, there are personal matters of opinion, disputable areas where God gives us personal freedom. But we are never at liberty to express our freedom in a way that causes others to stumble in sin. In all things, we want to show understanding, kindness, and love.

1 Corinthians 15:1–8; Romans 1:15–17;
Galatians 1:6–9; 2 Timothy 2:8; Ephesians 1:13–14;
4:4–6; Romans 8:9; 1 Corinthians 12:13;
1 Timothy 4:16; 2 Timothy 3:16–4:4;

Matthew 15:6–9; Acts 20:32; 1 Corinthians 11:1–2; 1 John 2:3–4; 2 Peter 3:14–16; Romans 14:1–23.

3. *The gospel.* We believe God created all things and made human beings in his image, so that we could enjoy a relationship with him and each other. But we lost our way, through Satan's influence. We are now spiritually dead, separated from God. Without his help, we gravitate toward sin and self-rule. The gospel is God's good news of reconciliation. It was promised to Abraham and David and revealed in Jesus' life, ministry, teaching, and sacrificial death on the cross. The gospel is the saving action of the triune God. The Father sent the Son into the world to take on human flesh and redeem us. Jesus came as the promised Messiah of the Old Testament. He ushered in the kingdom of God, died for our sins according to Scripture, was buried, and was raised on the third day. He defeated sin and death and ascended to heaven. He is seated at the right hand of God as Lord and he is coming back for his disciples. Through the Spirit, we are transformed and sanctified. God will raise everyone for the final judgment. Those who trusted and followed Jesus by faith will not experience punishment for their sins and separation from God in hell. Instead, we will join together with God in the renewal of all things in the consummated kingdom. We will live

together in the new heaven and new earth where we will glorify God and enjoy him forever.

> *Genesis 1–3; Romans 3:10–12; 7:8–25;*
> *Genesis 12:1–3; Galatians 3:6–9; Isaiah 11:1–4;*
> *2 Samuel 7:1–16; Micah 5:2–4; Daniel 2:44–45;*
> *Luke 1:33; John 1:1–3; Matthew 4:17;*
> *1 Corinthians 15:1–8; Acts 1:11; 2:36; 3:19–21;*
> *Colossians 3:1; Matthew 25:31–32; Revelation 21:1ff;*
> *Romans 3:21–26.*

4. *Faithful faith.* We believe that people are saved by grace through faith. The gospel of Jesus' kingdom calls people to both salvation and discipleship—no exceptions, no excuses. Faith is more than mere intellectual agreement or emotional warmth toward God. It is living and active; faith is surrendering our self-rule to the rule of God through Jesus in the power of the Spirit. We surrender by trusting and following Jesus as both Savior and Lord in all things. Faith includes allegiance, loyalty, and faithfulness to him.

> *Ephesians 2:8–9; Mark 8:34–38; Luke 14:25–35;*
> *Romans 1:3, 5; 16:25–26; Galatians 2:20;*
> *James 2:14–26; Matthew 7:21–23; Galatians 4:19;*
> *Matthew 28:19–20; 2 Corinthians 3:3, 17–18;*
> *Colossians 1:28.*

5. *New birth*. God so loved the world that he gave his one and only Son, that whoever believes in him shall not perish but have eternal life. To believe in Jesus means we trust and follow him as both Savior and Lord. When we commit to trust and follow Jesus, we express this faith by repenting from sin, confessing his name, and receiving baptism by immersion in water. Baptism, as an expression of faith, is for the remission of sins. We uphold baptism as the normative means of entry into the life of discipleship. It marks our commitment to regularly die to ourselves and rise to live for Christ in the power of the Holy Spirit. We believe God sovereignly saves as he sees fit, but we are bound by Scripture to uphold this teaching about surrendering to Jesus in faith through repentance, confession, and baptism.

> *1 Corinthians 8:6; John 3:1–9; 3:16–18;*
> *3:19–21; Luke 13:3–5; 24:46–47; Acts 2:38;*
> *3:19; 8:36–38; 16:31–33; 17:30; 20:21; 22:16;*
> *26:20; Galatians 3:26–27; Romans 6:1–4;*
> *10:9–10; 1 Peter 3:21; Romans 2:25–29;*
> *2 Chronicles 30:17–19; Matthew 28:19–20;*
> *Galatians 2:20; Acts 18:24–26.*

6. *Holy Spirit*. We believe God's desire is for everyone to be saved and come to the knowledge of the truth. Many hear the gospel but do not believe it because they

are blinded by Satan and resist the pull of the Holy Spirit. We encourage everyone to listen to the Word and let the Holy Spirit convict them of their sin and draw them into a relationship with God through Jesus. We believe that when we are born again and indwelt by the Holy Spirit, we are to live as people who are filled, empowered, and led by the Holy Spirit. This is how we walk with God and discern his voice. A prayerful life, rich in the Holy Spirit, is fundamental to true discipleship and living in step with the kingdom reign of Jesus. We seek to be a prayerful, Spirit-led fellowship.

> *1 Timothy 2:4; John 16:7–11; Acts 7:51;*
> *1 John 2:20, 27; John 3:5; Ephesians 1:13–14;*
> *5:18; Galatians 5:16–25; Romans 8:5–11;*
> *Acts 1:14; 2:42; 6:6; 9:40; 12:5; 13:3; 14:23; 20:36;*
> *2 Corinthians 3:3.*

7. *Disciple making.* We believe the core mission of the local church is making disciples of Jesus Christ—it is God's plan "A" to redeem the world and manifest the reign of his kingdom. We want to be disciples who make disciples because of our love for God and others. We personally seek to become more and more like Jesus through his Spirit so that Jesus would live through us. To help us focus on Jesus, his sacrifice on the cross, our unity in him, and his coming return, we typically share

communion in our weekly gatherings. We desire the fruits of biblical disciple making which are disciples who live and love like Jesus and "go" into every corner of society and to the ends of the earth. Disciple making is the engine that drives our missional service to those outside the church. We seek to be known where we live for the good that we do in our communities. We love and serve all people, as Jesus did, no strings attached. At the same time, as we do good for others, we also seek to form relational bridges that we prayerfully hope will open doors for teaching people the gospel of the kingdom and the way of salvation.

> *Matthew 28:19–20; Galatians 4:19;*
> *Acts 2:41; Philippians 1:20–21; Colossians 1:27–29;*
> *2 Corinthians 3:3; 1 Thessalonians 2:19–20;*
> *John 13:34–35; 1 John 3:16; 1 Corinthians 13:1–13;*
> *Luke 22:14–23; 1 Corinthians 11:17–24; Acts 20:7.*

8. *Kingdom life.* We believe in the present kingdom reign of God, the power of the Holy Spirit to transform people, and the priority of the local church. God's holiness should lead our churches to reject lifestyles characterized by pride, sexual immorality, homosexuality, easy divorce, idolatry, greed, materialism, gossip, slander, racism, violence, and the like. God's love should lead our churches to emphasize love as the distinguishing sign of

a true disciple. Love for one another should make the church like an extended family—a fellowship of married people, singles, elderly, and children who are all brothers and sisters to one another. The love of the extended church family to one another is vitally important. Love should be expressed in both service to the church and to the surrounding community. It leads to the breaking down of walls (racial, social, political), evangelism, acts of mercy, compassion, forgiveness, and the like. By demonstrating the ways of Jesus, the church reveals God's kingdom reign to the watching world.

1 Corinthians 1:2; Galatians 5:19–21;
Ephesians 5:3–7; Colossians 3:5–9;
Matthew 19:3–12; Romans 1:26–32; 14:17–18;
1 Peter 1:15–16; Matthew 25:31–46;
John 13:34–35; Colossians 3:12–13; 1 John 3:16;
1 Corinthians 13:1–13; 2 Corinthians 5:16–21.

9. *Counter-cultural living.* We believe Jesus' Lordship through Scripture will lead us to be a distinct light in the world. We follow the first and second Great Commandments where love and loyalty to God come first and love for others comes second. So we prioritize the gospel and one's relationship with God, with a strong commitment to love people in their secondary points of need too. The gospel is God's light for us. It teaches us

grace, mercy, and love. It also teaches us God's holiness, justice, and the reality of hell which led to Jesus' sacrifice of atonement for us. God's light is grace and truth, mercy and righteousness, love and holiness. God's light among us should be reflected in distinctive ways like the following:

A. We believe that human life begins at conception and ends upon natural death, and that all human life is priceless in the eyes of God. All humans should be treated as image-bearers of God. For this reason, we stand for the sanctity of life both at its beginning and its end. We oppose elective abortions and euthanasia as immoral and sinful. We understand that there are very rare circumstances that may lead to difficult choices when a mother or child's life is at stake, and we prayerfully surrender and defer to God's wisdom, grace, and mercy in those circumstances.

B. We believe God created marriage as the context for the expression and enjoyment of sexual relations. Jesus defines marriage as a covenant between one man and one woman. We believe that all sexual activity outside the bounds of marriage, including same-sex unions and same-sex marriage, are immoral and must not be condoned by disciples of Jesus.

C. We believe that Jesus invites all races and ethnicities into the kingdom of God. Because humanity has exhibited grave racial injustices throughout history, we believe that everyone, especially disciples, must be proactive in securing justice for people of all races and that racial reconciliation must be a priority for the church.

D. We believe that both men and women were created by God to equally reflect, in gendered ways, the nature and character of God in the world. In marriage, husbands and wives are to submit to one another, yet there are gender specific expressions: husbands model themselves in relationship with their wives after Jesus' sacrificial love for the church, and wives model themselves in relationship with their husbands after the church's willingness to follow Jesus. In the church, men and women serve as partners in the use of their gifts in ministry, while seeking to uphold New Testament norms which teach that the lead teacher/preacher role in the gathered church and the elder/overseer role are for qualified men. The vision of the Bible is an equal partnership of men and women in creation, in marriage, in salvation, in the gifts of the Spirit, and in the ministries of the church but exercised in ways that honor gender as described in the Bible.

E. We believe that we must resist the forces of culture that focus on materialism and greed. The Bible teaches that the love of money is the root of all sorts of evil and that greed is idolatry. Disciples of Jesus should joyfully give liberally and work sacrificially for the poor, the marginalized, and the oppressed.

Romans 12:3–8; Matthew 22:36–40; 1 Corinthians 12:4–7; Ephesians 2:10; 4:11–13; 1 Peter 4:10–11; Matthew 20:24–27; Philippians 1:1; Acts 20:28; 1 Timothy 2:11–15; 3:1–7; Titus 1:5–9; 1 Corinthians 11:2–9; 14:33–36; Ephesians 5:21–33; Colossians 3:18–19; 1 Corinthians 7:32–35.

10. *The end.* We believe that Jesus is coming back to earth in order to bring this age to an end. Jesus will reward the saved and punish the wicked, and finally destroy God's last enemy, death. He will put all things under the Father, so that God may be all in all forever. That is why we have urgency for the Great Commission—to make disciples of all nations. We like to look at the Great Commission as an inherent part of God's original command to "be fruitful and multiply."

We want to be disciples of Jesus who love people and help them to be disciples of Jesus. We are a movement of disciples who make disciples who help renew existing churches and who start new churches that make more disciples. We want to reach as many as possible—until Jesus returns and God restores all creation to himself in the new heaven and new earth.

Matthew 25:31–32; Acts 17:31; Revelation 20:11–15;
2 Thessalonians 1:6–10; Mark 9:43–49;
Luke 12:4–7; Acts 4:12; John 14:6; Luke 24:46–48;
Matthew 28:19–20; Genesis 12:1–3; Galatians 2:20;
4:19; Luke 6:40; Luke 19:10; Revelation 21:1ff.

NOTES

1. For a Renew.org resource that zeroes in on the topic of baptism (whereas this volume describes the new birth as a whole), see Tony Twist, Bobby Harrington, and David Young, *Baptism: What the Bible Teaches* (Renew.org, 2018).

2. E. A. Livingstone, *Oxford Concise Dictionary of the Christian Church* (New York: Oxford University Press, 2006), 143.

3. C. Marvin Pate, *The Writings of John* (Grand Rapids: Zondervan, 2011), 48.

4. Matthew W. Bates, *Salvation by Allegiance Alone: Rethinking Faith, Works, and the Gospel of Jesus the King* (Grand Rapids: Baker Academic, 2017), 83.

5. Bates, 83.

6. Bates, 109.

7. Owen Olbricht, *Baptism: A Response of Faith* (Delight, AR: Gospel Light Publishing Company, 200), 45–46.

8. Martin Luther, quoted by Karl Barth, *The Epistle to the Romans*, trans. Edwyn C. Hoskyns (London: Oxford, 1933), 96.

9. See Mark E. Moore, *Faithful Faith: Reclaiming Faith from Culture and Tradition* (Renew.org, 2021).

10. Olbricht, 42.

11. *Theological Dictionary of the New Testament*, ed. Gerhard Kittel and Gerhard Friedrich, trans. Geoffry W. Bromiley (Grand Rapids: Eerdmans, 1964–1976), 4:975–1003. The Jewish historian Josephus and the Jewish philosopher Philo of Alexandria both used *metanoia* in a sense of a change heart and behavior, as opposed to the pagan Greek idea that "never suggests an alteration in the total moral attitude, a profound change in life's direction, a conversion which affects the whole conduct." See *TDNT*, 4:979.

12. Hicks and Taylor, 168.

13. Michael J. Ovey bluntly states that the twenty-first century is "a time of repentanceless Christianity" in the Western world. See his *The Feasts of Repentance: From Luke–Acts to Systematic and Pastoral Theology*, New Studies in Biblical Theology (Downers Grove, IL: InterVarsity Press, 2009), 1.

14. Scot McKnight, *The Letter of James*, The New International Commentary on the New Testament (Grand Rapids: Eerdmans Publishing Company, 2011), 353.

15. For an in-depth look at how repentance and forgiveness build Christian community, see Miroslav Volf, *Free of Charge: Giving and Forgiving in a Culture Stripped of Grace* (Grand Rapids: Zondervan, 2009).

16. This quote comes from one of the earliest extant non-biblical Christian documents, 2 Clement 9:6–8. Some think it was written by the early church leader Clement of Rome, while others consider it an early Christian sermon. Either way, it was clearly written by a Christian in the late first or early second century. This translation comes from Michael W. Holmes, *The Apostolic Fathers: Greek Texts and English Translations*, 3rd ed. (Grand Rapids: Baker Academic, 2007), 149.

17. Karl Barth, *The Teaching of the Church Regarding Baptism*, trans. Ernest A. Payne (London: SCM, 1948), 31.

18. This is where the so-called "sinner's prayer" gets it right, in that it involves confessing sin and confessing to belief in Jesus. However, such a prayer is never found in the Bible. While the New Testament supports confession of Christ, baptism is the appropriate response connected with this confession, not prayer.

19. See D. A. Carson, *Jesus the Son of God: A Christological Title Often Overlooked, Sometimes Misunderstood, and Currently Disputed* (Wheaton, IL: Crossway, 2013). See also the confession of Jesus as king made by the repentant thief on the cross, who said to

Jesus, "Jesus, remember me when you come into your kingdom" (Luke 23:42).

20. *TDNT,* 3:1056.

21. *Kurios* is used of God some six thousand times in the Greek version of the Old Testament. See also C. E. Cranfield, *A Critical and Exegetical Commentary on the Epistle to the Romans,* vol. 2 (Edinburgh: T&T Clark International), 529.

22. The Latin term Augustus used was *divi filius.*

23. See, for example, Wright's chapter "Paul's Gospel and Caesar's Empire," in *Paul and Politics, Ekklesia, Israel, Imperium, Interpretation: Essays in Honor of Krister Stendahl,* ed. Richard A. Horsley (Harrisburg: Trinity Press International, 2000), 160–183.

24. Paul Hartog, *Polycarp's Epistle to the Philippians and the Martyrdom of Polycarp: Introduction, Text, and Commentary* (Oxford: Oxford University Press, 2013), 251.

25. Hartog, 253.

26. Acts of Justin 2, recension B. As quoted in Everett Ferguson, *The Rule of Faith: A Guide* (Eugene: Cascade Books, 2015), 3.

27. See Chapter 1 for a fuller discussion of this.

28. Leonard J. Vander Zee, *Christ, Baptism and the Lord's Supper: Recovering the Sacraments for Evangelical Worship* (Downers Grove, IL: InterVarsity Press, 2004), 80.

29. "The Nicene Creed" in *Documents of the Christian Church*, ed. Henry Bettenson and Chris Maunder (Oxford: Oxford University Press, 1999), 29.

30. G. Walter Hansen, *Galatians* (Downers Grove, IL: IVP Academic, 2010), 101.

31. James Strong, *Strong's Expanded Exhaustive Concordance of the Bible,* (Nashville: Thomas Nelson, 2009), #4982.

32. *Strong's,* #863.

33. CCC #1257.

34. Walter Bauer, *A Greek-English Lexicon of the New Testament and Other Early Christian Literature*, 2nd ed. (Chicago: University of Chicago Press, 1958), 131.

35. John Mark Hicks and Greg Taylor, *Down in the River to Pray* (Siloam Springs, AR: Leafwood Publishers, 2004), 96.

36. Hicks and Taylor, 94.

37. Stanley Grenz, *Theology for the Community of God* (Grand Rapids: Eerdmans, 1994), 433.

38. Olbricht, 128.

39. As quoted in Eric E. Peterson, *Wade in the Water: Following the Sacred Stream of Baptism* (Eugene: Cascade Books, 2018), 79.

40. C. S. Lewis, *Miracles: A Preliminary Study* (London: The Centenary Press, 1947), 117.